LET'S CELEBRATE!

Make Me Laugh!

LET'S CELEBRATE!

jokes about holidays

by Peter & Connie Roop / pictures by Joan Hanson

Lerner Publications Company · Minneapolis

For Mother and Father, who make life a celebration!

This book is available in two editions:
Library binding by Lerner Publications Company
Soft cover by First Avenue Editions
241 First Avenue North
Minneapolis, Minnesota 55401

Library of Congress Cataloging-in-Publication Data

Roop, Peter.
   Let's celebrate!

   (Make me laugh!)
   Summary: A collection of jokes and riddles about
holidays, including "What is a wolf's favorite holiday?
Howl-oween."
   1. Holidays—Juvenile humor. 2. Wit and humor,
Juvenile. [1. Holidays—Wit and humor. 2. Jokes.
3. Riddles] I. Roop, Connie. II. Hanson, Joan, ill.
III. Title. IV. Series.
PN6231.H547R66   1986   818'.5402   86-7247
ISBN 0-8225-0989-X (lib. bdg.)
ISBN 0-8225-9529-X (pbk.)

Manufactured in the United States of America

   3   4   5   6   7   8   9   10   96   95   94   93   92   91   90   89   88

Q: What is the best thing to put in a birthday cake?

A: Your teeth.

Q: What do cats say on New Year's Eve?
A: "Happy Mew Year."

Q: When do pigs like to play in the dirt?
A: Ground Hog's Day.

Q: What did Abraham Lincoln do with his
boots after he wore them out?
A: He wore them back in again.

Q: What is a pig's favorite holiday?
A: Valen-swine's Day.

Q: What happens when two valentines fight?

A: A heart is broken.

Q: Why was cupid put in jail?
A: He was caught stealing hearts.

Q: What does a baseball pitcher do on his birthday?
A: He throws a party.

Q: Why are goats fun to have at a party?
A: They are always kidding around.

Q: Why did the goat crash the party?
A: She was always butting in.

Q: Why is a pig's birthday party so much fun?
A: Everyone goes hog wild.

Q: Which burns longer, candles on a birthday cake or candles in a candlestick?
A: Neither, they both burn shorter.

Q: What did one birthday candle say to the other?
A: "These birthdays really burn me up!"

Q: What do rabbits say at Easter?
A: "Hoppy Easter."

Q: What do you say to a lazy Easter bunny?
A: "Hop to it!"

Q: What is an Easter bunny's favorite sandwich?
A: Peanut butter and jelly beans.

Q: Why did the boy carry a gun on Easter morning?
A: He was hunting for Easter eggs.

Q: What does an Easter bunny grow in his garden?

A: Jelly beans.

Q: Why is Easter dinner fun?
A: People ham it up.

Q: What is a kangaroo's favorite time of year?
A: Spring.

Q: What is the best month for a parade?
A: March.

Q: Why is Father's Day later in the year than Mother's Day?
A: It's "father" away.

Q: What are three good things about school?
A: June, July, and August.

Q: What is the best day to wave?
A: Flag Day.

Q: How do cows keep track of holidays?
A: With a cow-lendar.

Q: What do you drink at a parade?
A: Floats.

Q: Where was the Declaration of
Independence signed?
A: At the bottom.

Sally: How was your Fourth of July?
Tony: It was a blast.

Q: What do you eat with soup on the
Fourth of July?
A: Fire crackers.

Q: What makes more noise than a firecracker?
A: Two firecrackers.

Q: When is a firecracker no longer a
firecracker?
A: When it's ablaze.

Q: What does a firecracker do when it's angry?

A: Blows its top.

Q: What do hogs do on Labor Day?
A: Go on pig-nics.

Q: What was the first bus to cross the ocean?
A: Colum-bus.

Q: Where do you go to celebrate Election Day?
A: Political parties.

Q: Why did Holly miss school on her birthday?
A: She heard it was a Holly-day.

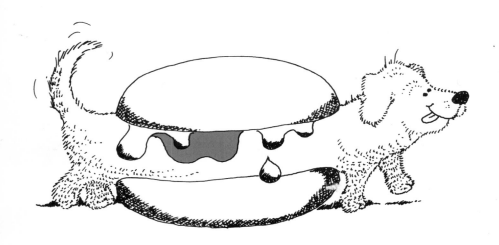

Q: What do you call a hungry dachshund
in October?

A: A hollow-weenie.

Q: What is a wolf's favorite holiday?
A: Howl-oween.

Q: What kind of tape do you use
on Halloween?
A: Mask-ing tape.

Q: What do you find at the beach on
Halloween?
A: Sand-witches.

Q: How does a witch tell time?
A: She checks her witch watch.

Q: What plays baseball on Halloween?
A: A baseball bat.

Q: What kind of key do you use on
    Thanksgiving?
A: A tur-key.

Q: What kind of music did the Pilgrims like?
A: Plymouth rock.

Q: What was the turkey doing in the
    Thanksgiving Day parade?
A: Using his drumsticks.

Q: Why is turkey a good holiday food?
A: You can gobble it up.

Q: Why were the cranberries red?
A: They saw the turkey dressing.

Mother: How did you feel after the feast?
Daughter: Aw-full.

Q: What did Santa say on Christmas Eve?
A: "That wraps it up for another year."

Q: What do you find at the beach
at Christmas?
A: Sandy claws.

Knock, knock.
Who's there?
Santa.
Santa, who?
Santa letter, didn't you?

Mark: Why is Rudolph the Red a good
weatherman?
Sally: Why?
Mark: Rudolph the Red knows rain, dear.

Q: How do you know when an elephant is going on vacation?

A: He packs his trunk.

ABOUT THE AUTHORS

PETER AND CONNIE ROOP have enjoyed sharing jokes with students in the United States and Great Britain. When not joking around, Peter and Connie write books and articles. Traveling, camping, and reading with their children, Sterling and Heidi, are their favorite pastimes. Both graduates of Lawrence University, the Roops now live in Appleton, Wisconsin.

ABOUT THE ARTIST

JOAN HANSON lives with her husband and two sons in Afton, Minnesota. Her distinctive, deliberately whimsical pen-and-ink drawings have illustrated more than 30 children's books. Ms. Hanson is also an accomplished weaver. A graduate of Carleton College, Hanson enjoys tennis, skiing, sailing, reading, traveling, and walking in the woods surrounding her home.

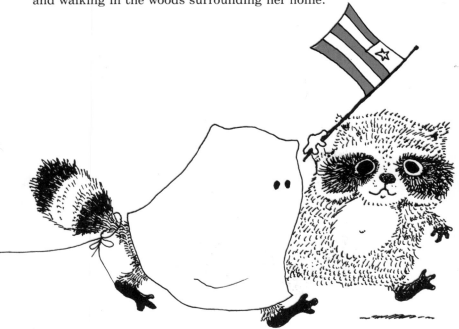

Make Me Laugh!

101 ANIMAL JOKES
101 FAMILY JOKES
101 KNOCK-KNOCK JOKES
101 MONSTER JOKES
101 SCHOOL JOKES
101 SPORTS JOKES
CAT'S OUT OF THE BAG!
DUMB CLUCKS!
ELEPHANTS NEVER FORGET!
FACE THE MUSIC!
GO HOG WILD!
GOING BUGGY!

GRIN AND BEAR IT!
IN THE DOGHOUSE!
LET'S CELEBRATE!
OUT TO LUNCH!
OUT TO PASTURE!
SNAKES ALIVE!
SOMETHING'S FISHY!
SPACE OUT!
STICK OUT YOUR TONGUE!
WHAT'S YOUR NAME?
WHAT'S YOUR NAME, AGAIN?